HOW TO SELL ON EBAY FOR BEGINNERS 2024

Unlock Your Online Success and Master the Art of Selling on eBay with Tips and Strategies for Beginners in 2024

SUSAN HARRISON

Copyright © 2024 by Susan Harrison

All rights reserved. No part of this publication may be reproduced, distributed, or transmitted in any form or by any means, including photocopying, recording, or other electronic or mechanical methods, without the prior written permission of the publisher, except in the case of brief quotations embodied in critical reviews and certain other noncommercial uses permitted by copyright law.

Contents

Introduction 5
Understanding the eBay marketplace 8
    Navigating the Marketplace 10
    Benefits and Drawbacks of selling on eBay 11
    Identifying Your Niche and Target Audience 14
Creating an eBay Account and Verifying Your Identity 18
    Creating an eBay Account 18
    Verifying Your Identity 20
    Navigating the eBay Interface 22
    Choosing Between Personal and Business Accounts 26
Building Your Seller Reputation 30
    Understanding Feedback and Maintaining a Positive Rating 34
    Policies and Practices for Building Trust with Buyers .. 37
Finding Treasure in Your Closet: Sourcing Products to Sell 41
    Understanding Market Trends and Researching Your Competition 44
    Ethical Sourcing 46
    eBay Restricted Items Policy Overview 51
Crafting Listings that Convert 53
    Writing Eye-Catching Titles 55
    Writing Detailed Descriptions 57
    Optimizing for Search with Keyword Research 63
    Using High-Quality Pictures and Videos to Showcase Your Products 65
    How to take a good product photos 70

- Pricing to Win: Profitable Strategies for Beginners 75
  - Understanding Fees and Calculating Your Bottom Line 76
  - Calculating Your Bottom Line 79
  - Setting Competitive Prices with Auction Formats or Buy It Now 80
  - Promotions and Discounts to Attract Buyers and Boost Sales 84
- Shipping and Delivery Made Easy 88
  - Choosing the Right Methods and Costs 88
  - Packaging Your Products for Safe and Happy Deliveries 92
  - A Guide to International Shipping on eBay 95
- Customer Service 101 (Building Trust and Handling Inquiries) 98
  - Addressing Buyer Concerns and Handling Disputes .. 100
  - Building Repeat Customers and Cultivating Positive Relationships 105
- Tools and Technology to Simplify Your Sales Journey 107
  - Inventory Management and Listing Automation for Efficiency 107
- Conclusion 113

Thank you for choosing my book and embarking on this eBay journey together. This bonus content is my way of expressing gratitude and providing you with insights and strategies to thrive in the dynamic world of eBay selling.

SCAN THIS CODE TO ACCESS THE BONUS

Introduction

Remember that dusty box of "maybe one day" sweaters in the attic? Or the collection of vintage video games gathering cobwebs in the basement? Yeah, I get it. We all have them – those forgotten treasures collecting dust instead of generating cash. But what if I told you those piles of "stuff" could be your passport to financial freedom?

My name is Susan, and eBay isn't just a website – it's my entrepreneurial playground. Five years ago, I was that person with the cluttered attic, drowning in "stuff" and wishing for financial relief. Enter eBay. With a healthy dose of skepticism and a thirst for adventure, I started listing a few items. To my surprise, they sold (and quickly!). Before I knew it, I was hooked, transforming my clutter into a thriving online business.

This book isn't just a how-to manual, it's a map to unlock the hidden potential of your own "maybe one day" treasures. Forget those boring business guides – I'm your real-life guide, sharing the hard-won lessons, secret strategies, and hilarious mishaps that turned me from a garage-sale enthusiast into a bona fide eBay success story.

For 2024, this book has been updated to cover the latest platform updates, hottest selling categories, and effective strategies for navigating the ever-evolving world of online auctions. Whether you're a seasoned collector or a complete newbie, this book will equip you with the knowledge and tools to turn your clutter into a cash-generating machine. We'll navigate the ins and outs of listing, pricing, shipping, and customer service, all real-world examples.

Speaking of unique items, let me tell you about the time I stumbled upon a vintage typewriter at a flea market. It was a beautiful Art Deco model, dusty but with potential. I listed it on eBay, highlighting its unique features and excellent condition. The challenge? The typewriter was quite heavy and shipping costs seemed daunting. So, I got creative, offering local pickup as an option and emphasizing the potential value for collectors. To my surprise, a bidding war erupted, and the typewriter sold for significantly more than I anticipated! The buyer, a history buff, was thrilled with his new acquisition, and I learned a valuable lesson about the power of niche markets and targeted marketing.

So dust off those "maybe one day" treasures, grab your phone, and get ready to join me on a journey from cluttered closets to online success. Trust me, the thrill of turning forgotten relics into profit is unlike anything you've ever experienced. Let's unlock the treasure chest of opportunity right inside your home and pave your path to eBay profitability, one listing at a time!

CHAPTER 1

Understanding the eBay marketplace

Before you start listing your "maybe one day" items and turning them into cold, hard cash, let's take a moment to understand the exciting world of this online marketplace.

What is eBay?

At its core, eBay is an online platform that connects buyers and sellers from all over the globe. Founded in 1995 by Pierre Omidyar, it started as a simple auction platform but has since evolved into a multifaceted marketplace offering a variety of buying and selling options. You can find practically anything on eBay, from vintage collectibles and electronics to clothing, furniture, and even cars!

A Brief History of eBay:

- 1995: The journey begins as a website called "AuctionWeb," where Omidyar

sells a broken laser pointer (fun fact: it went for $14.83!).
- 1997: The name changes to eBay, and the platform gains traction, attracting millions of users.
- 2002: eBay acquires PayPal, solidifying its position as a leader in online transactions.
- 2008: The Company expands globally, establishing marketplaces in various countries.
- 2024: Today, eBay boasts over 195 million active buyers worldwide, facilitating billions of dollars in transactions annually.

eBay operates on the foundation of auctions and fixed-price listings, offering sellers the flexibility to choose their preferred selling format. With categories ranging from electronics and fashion to collectibles and more, eBay caters to a vast spectrum of interests. It's not just a transactional platform; it's a dynamic community where buyers and sellers converge.

While auctions remain a core part of eBay's identity, the platform offers several other selling formats to cater to diverse needs:

- Buy It Now: List items at a fixed price for immediate purchase.
- Best Offer: Allow buyers to submit offers on your listing.
- Classifieds: Advertise locally within your area.

Navigating the Marketplace

Understanding the key components of eBay will make your experience smoother:

- Search Engine: Find specific items using keywords, filters, and sorting options.
- Categories & Subcategories: Browse through a vast array of products organized by category.
- Seller Profiles & Feedback: Check seller feedback ratings to assess their trustworthiness.
- Watchlists & Saved Searches: Keep track of interesting items and searches.

- Bidding & Buying: Understand auction rules, bidding strategies, and buying processes.

Benefits and Drawbacks of selling on eBay

Before diving headfirst into your eBay selling adventure, it's wise to consider both the exciting opportunities and potential challenges you might encounter.

<u>Benefits:</u>

- Vast Audience: Reach millions of potential buyers worldwide, increasing your chances of selling your items.
- Wide Variety of Products: Sell practically anything that's legal and allowed by eBay's policies.
- Flexible Selling Formats: Choose between auctions, fixed-price listings, or "Best Offer" options to suit your preferences.
- Global Reach: Expand your selling potential to international markets (with

considerations for shipping and regulations).
- Low Startup Costs: No physical store needed, minimizing overhead expenses compared to traditional businesses.
- Scalability: Start small and gradually grow your business as you gain experience and success.
- Community Support: Access a wealth of resources, tutorials, and forums for seller support and networking.
- Potential for High Profits: Reach a wider audience and potentially earn more compared to local garage sales or classifieds.

Drawbacks:

- Fees: eBay charges insertion fees, final value fees, and payment processing fees, impacting your profit margins.
- Competition: Face competition from other sellers, requiring competitive pricing and strategic marketing.
- Scams and Fraud: Be aware of potential scams and take necessary precautions to protect yourself.

- Shipping Hassles: Packing, shipping, and managing returns can add complexity and costs.
- Customer Service: Be prepared to handle customer inquiries, complaints, and potential disputes professionally.
- Time Commitment: Maintaining a successful eBay business requires time and effort for listing, managing orders, and marketing.
- Learning Curve: Understanding eBay's policies, best practices, and effective selling strategies takes time and continuous learning.

Identifying Your Niche and Target Audience

Congratulations on taking the first steps towards your eBay selling adventure! Now it's time to embark on a crucial quest: discovering your niche and target audience. Just like Aladdin wouldn't have found the magic lamp without knowing where to look, pinpointing your niche ensures you attract the right buyers and maximize your selling potential.

What is a Niche?

Imagine a vast marketplace filled with diverse items. Your niche is your cozy corner within that marketplace, specializing in a specific category or sub-category that aligns with your interests, expertise, and target audience. It's your unique selling proposition, setting you apart from the general crowd.

Why is Finding Your Niche Important?

- Focus: By specializing, you gain deeper knowledge of your products, allowing you to source, price, and market them more effectively.

- Competition: In a smaller niche, you face less competition, making it easier to stand out and attract buyers.
- Profitability: Understanding your niche's trends and demands helps you price competitively and potentially earn higher profits.
- Sustainability: A well-defined niche fosters repeat customers and builds brand loyalty within your targeted community.

How to Identify Your Niche:

1. Explore Your Passions: What are you genuinely interested in? What knowledge or skills do you possess? Consider collectibles, hobbies, crafts, or anything that sparks your enthusiasm.
2. Market Research: Dive into eBay categories, trending searches, and competitor analysis to identify in-demand niches with potential. Tools like Terapeak and Sellbrite can provide valuable insights.
3. Consider Your Resources: Assess your budget, storage space, and sourcing

capabilities. Choose a niche that aligns with your resources and avoids overly saturated or restricted categories.
4. Experiment and Refine: Start small and experiment with different niches. Track your progress, analyze results, and adapt your approach based on what resonates with buyers.

Identifying Your Target Audience:

Once you've identified your niche, it's time to understand who you're selling to. Your target audience is the specific group of people most likely to be interested in buying your products.

Key Questions to Ask:

- Demographics: Age, gender, location, income level, etc.
- Interests: Hobbies, lifestyles, online behavior, etc.
- Needs and Pain Points: What problems do they face? What solutions do your products offer?
- Buying Habits: Where do they shop online? What influences their purchasing decisions?

Benefits of Knowing Your Target Audience:

- Targeted Marketing: Craft messaging and visuals that resonate directly with your ideal buyers.
- Product Selection: Tailor your offerings to their specific needs and preferences.
- Pricing Strategy: Set competitive prices based on their perceived value and buying power.
- Customer Service: Provide personalized communication and support that resonates with their expectations.

Researching Your Target Audience:

- Online communities and forums: Connect with groups relevant to your niche and observe their discussions.
- Social media: Analyze demographics and interests of people engaging with similar products or brands.
- Surveys and questionnaires: Gather direct feedback from potential customers within your target audience

CHAPTER 2

Creating an eBay Account and Verifying Your Identity

Now that you've identified your niche and target audience, it's time to officially join the eBay community! This chapter will guide you through the seamless process of creating your eBay account and verifying your identity

Creating an eBay Account

1. Visit eBay Website:
    o Open your web browser and go to the eBay website (www.ebay.com).
2. Sign Up:
    o Click on the "Sign In" or "Register" button, usually located at the top of the eBay homepage.

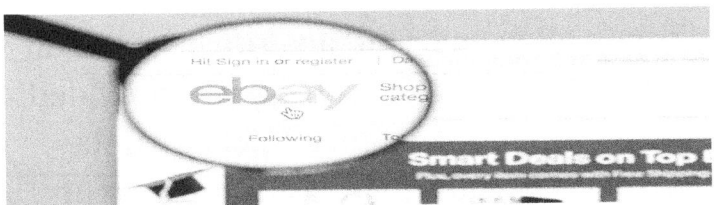

3. Enter Your Information:
    - Fill in the required information, including your first and last name, email address, and a secure password.
    - Alternatively, you can simplify the process by clicking "Continue with Facebook" or "Continue with Google" if you prefer to register using your existing Facebook or Google account.
    - Click "Create account."

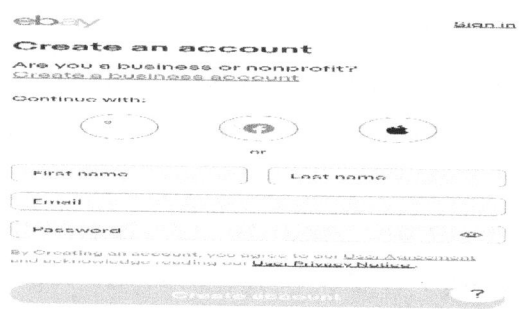

4. Verify Email:
    - eBay will send a verification email to the email address you provided.
    - Open the email and click on the verification link to confirm your registration.

Verifying Your Identity

eBay takes security seriously, and verifying your identity ensures a safe and trustworthy platform for everyone. Verification steps may vary depending on your location and selling activity, but common methods include:

1. Provide Personal Information:
    - After creating your eBay account, you may be prompted to provide additional personal information, such as your address and phone number.
2. Link PayPal Account (Optional):
    - While not mandatory, linking a PayPal account can facilitate transactions. Follow the prompts to link your PayPal account if you have one.
3. Verify Identity:
    - eBay may require identity verification for security purposes. This could involve confirming your identity through methods like phone verification or asking for additional documentation.

4. Phone Verification:
    - You may receive a code via text or a phone call to verify your phone number. Enter the code on the verification page.
5. Document Verification:
    - In some cases, eBay may request documents, such as a photo ID, to verify your identity. Follow the instructions to upload the necessary documents securely.
6. Two-Step Verification (Optional):
    - Enhance account security by enabling two-step verification. This typically involves receiving a code on your phone for additional login security.
7. Review and Confirm:
    - Review all provided information, ensuring accuracy and completeness.
    - Confirm that you agree to eBay's terms and conditions.
8. Complete the Process:
    - Once your identity is verified, you'll receive a confirmation, and your eBay account is ready for use.

Navigating the eBay Interface

You've created your account, verified your identity, and are now ready to dive deeper into the exciting world of online selling. Buckle up as we explore the eBay interface and essential tools that will empower you to list your items, manage your business, and navigate the marketplace with confidence.

1. Homepage:
    - Upon logging in, you'll land on the eBay homepage. Here, you'll find featured items, promotions, and personalized recommendations based on your activity.
2. Search Bar:
    - Use the search bar to look for specific items, categories, or sellers. Advanced search options can help refine your results.
3. Categories:
    - Explore specific categories by hovering over the "Shop by

category" menu. This is a quick way to find items related to your interests.
4. Your eBay:
   - Access your personal eBay hub by clicking on "My eBay." Here, you can view your buying and selling activities, messages, and saved items.
5. Messages:
   - Keep track of communication with buyers and sellers in the Messages section. It's an essential tool for managing transactions.
6. Buying and Selling:
   - Use the "Buy" and "Sell" options to navigate through the buying and selling processes. These sections provide access to your shopping cart, watchlist, and selling activities.
7. Watchlist:
   - Add items to your watchlist to monitor prices and auctions. It's a useful tool for staying updated on items you're interested in.
8. Saved Searches:

- Save your favorite searches to receive notifications when new items matching your criteria are listed.

Utilizing eBay Tools

1. Advanced Search:
    - Utilize the advanced search features to narrow down your search results based on price range, location, seller rating, and more.
2. Filters:
    - Refine your search results using filters like item condition, location, and seller type.
3. Best Offer:
    - When selling, consider using the "Best Offer" option to allow buyers to negotiate prices.
4. eBay App:
    - Download the eBay mobile app for convenient access, real-time notifications, and the ability to manage your account on the go.

5. Seller Hub:
   - Sellers can use the Seller Hub to track sales, manage listings, and gain insights into their business performance.
6. Feedback System:
   - The feedback system is crucial for building a trustworthy profile. Leave feedback for your transactions, and check a seller's or buyer's feedback before engaging in a transaction.
7. Shipping Tools:
   - Sellers can utilize eBay's shipping tools to calculate shipping costs, print shipping labels, and manage the shipping process efficiently.
8. Customer Support:
   - Access eBay's customer support for assistance with account issues, disputes, or general inquiries.

By familiarizing yourself with these interface elements and tools, you'll navigate eBay confidently and make the most of your buying and selling experiences.

Choosing Between Personal and Business Accounts

Congratulations on navigating the eBay interface and mastering the essential tools! Now, it's time to make a crucial decision: **choosing the right account type for your selling journey**. Understanding the differences between **Personal and Business accounts** will equip you to select the option that best aligns with your goals, resources, and selling aspirations.

Personal Account:

- Ideal for: Casual sellers, individuals decluttering their belongings, or those testing the waters of online selling.
- Limitations:
    - Listing limit of 10 active fixed-price or auction listings per month.
    - Lower selling limits on certain categories.
    - Fewer payment processing options.

- - Limited access to advanced selling tools and features.
- Benefits:
  - Free to set up and maintain.
  - Simple and straightforward to use.
  - No additional verification required.

Business Account:

- Ideal for: Serious sellers, entrepreneurs, and businesses looking to scale their online sales.
- Features:
  - Higher listing limits and selling thresholds.
  - Access to a wider range of payment processing options.
  - Advanced selling tools and features, including store subscriptions, marketing tools, and bulk listing options.
  - Ability to accept international payments.
  - Potential tax benefits (consult with a tax professional).
- Costs:

- Monthly subscription fee (varies depending on chosen plan).
- Higher insertion fees for listings.

Deciding Factor: Consider These Questions:

Selling Volume: How many items do you plan to sell per month?
Selling Goals: Are you looking to make a few extra bucks or build a sustainable business?
Investment: Are you willing to invest in a monthly subscription for advanced features?
Payment Processing: Do you need access to specific payment options or international transactions?
Tax Implications: Consult with a tax professional to understand potential benefits of a business account.

Remember: There's no one-size-fits-all answer. Choose the account type that aligns with your current needs and future aspirations. You can always switch between Personal and Business accounts later as your selling activity evolves.

CHAPTER 3

Building Your Seller Reputation

Congratulations on choosing your account type and setting sail on your eBay adventure! Now, it's time to shine a spotlight on your unique identity within the vast marketplace. Your seller profile serves as your online storefront, making a crucial first impression on potential buyers and building trust in your brand. Let's dive into the secrets of crafting a compelling profile that attracts customers and converts them into loyal fans.

The Essential Elements:

1. Profile Picture:

- Upload a clear and professional profile picture. This could be a headshot or a logo if you're running a business. A visual representation helps buyers connect with you.

2. Username:

- Choose a username that reflects your identity or brand. Make it memorable and easy to spell. Avoid using symbols or numbers that may complicate recall.

3. About Me/Bio:

- Use the "About Me" section to share a brief and personable introduction. Highlight your passion for what you sell, your expertise, or any unique qualities that set you apart.

4. Business Information (For Business Accounts):

- If you have a business account, provide essential business information such as your company name, address, and contact details. This adds a layer of transparency and professionalism.

5. Seller Policies:

- Clearly outline your selling policies. Cover aspects like shipping times, return policies, and any specific terms buyers should be aware of. This helps manage expectations and build trust.

6. Feedback and Ratings:

- Showcase your positive feedback and high ratings. Buyers often look at feedback to gauge a seller's reputation. Provide excellent customer service to accumulate positive reviews.

7. Customize Your Storefront (For Business Accounts):

- If you have a business account, take advantage of eBay's customization options for your storefront. Include a banner, logo, and other visuals that represent your brand.

8. Specializations and Expertise:

- Highlight any specializations or unique expertise you bring to your selling. If you're knowledgeable about specific products, let buyers know.

9. Contact Information:

- Ensure your contact information is accurate and up-to-date. This includes your email address and any other contact details you choose to provide.

10. Promotions and Discounts (For Business Accounts):

- If applicable, mention any ongoing promotions, discounts, or exclusive deals. This can entice buyers and encourage them to explore your listings.

11. Responsive Communication:

- Emphasize your commitment to responsive communication. Let buyers know that you're available to answer questions and address concerns promptly.

12. Customer Testimonials (if available):

- If you have received positive testimonials from previous customers, consider including excerpts or summaries in your profile. This adds authenticity to your reputation.

Beyond the Basics:

- Visual Appeal: Enhance your profile with a personalized banner or logo (available for Business accounts).
- Storytelling: Share anecdotes about your passion for your niche or the origin of your items to connect with buyers on an emotional level.
- Community Engagement: Participate in relevant forums and discussions to showcase your expertise and build relationships with potential customers.
- Promotions and Offers: Highlight ongoing promotions or special offers to attract attention and incentivize purchases.

Understanding Feedback and Maintaining a Positive Rating

Building trust and maintaining a positive seller rating are crucial aspects of long-term success on the platform.

What is Feedback and Why is it Important?

Feedback is a two-way communication system on eBay where buyers can rate their experience with you as a seller. It consists of a star rating (from 1 to 5, with 5 being the highest) and an optional comment section where buyers can share their thoughts on various aspects, such as product accuracy, communication, shipping speed, and overall satisfaction.

Positive feedback is your golden ticket to success. It signifies to potential buyers that you're a trustworthy and reliable seller, encouraging them to purchase from you with confidence. Conversely, negative feedback can act as a deterrent, raising doubts and potentially harming your sales.

1. Feedback Score:
    - Your feedback score is a numerical representation of your reputation on eBay. It's calculated based on the feedback you receive from buyers.
2. Detailed Seller Ratings (DSRs):

- In addition to written feedback, buyers can provide detailed seller ratings in categories like communication, shipping time, and item description. Consistently high DSRs contribute to a positive reputation.
3. Feedback Percentage:
    - Your feedback percentage is the ratio of positive feedback received to the total number of feedback received. Aim for a high percentage to build trust with potential buyers.

How to Encourage Positive Feedback:

- Prioritize Customer Satisfaction: Strive to exceed buyer expectations at every step, from accurate product descriptions to prompt communication and efficient shipping.
- Communicate Proactively: Keep buyers informed throughout the transaction, promptly answer questions, and address any concerns with courtesy and professionalism.

- Resolve Issues Amicably: Mistakes happen, but how you handle them matters. Be responsive, understanding, and offer fair solutions to any problems that may arise.
- Go the Extra Mile: Consider adding small gestures of appreciation, such as handwritten thank-you notes or bonus items, to delight your customers and create a memorable experience.
- Request Feedback Politely: Remind buyers to leave feedback after completing their purchase, but avoid being pushy or demanding.

Policies and Practices for Building Trust with Buyers

We'll explore key policies and practices that foster a transparent and reliable environment, ultimately attracting customers and propelling your business forward.

Transparency is Key:

- Accurate Listings: Meticulously describe your items, highlighting any

imperfections or wear and tear. Use high-quality photos from various angles to depict the product accurately.
- Clear Pricing: State your price upfront, including any additional fees or taxes. Avoid hidden charges or misleading price structures.
- Honest Communication: Promptly respond to buyer inquiries and messages, providing accurate and informative answers. Be upfront about any potential delays or challenges.
- Realistic Shipping Details: Clearly outline shipping costs, timelines, and policies. Stick to your estimated shipping times and promptly communicate any unforeseen delays.

Policies that Build Confidence:

- Fair Return Policy: Establish a reasonable return policy that aligns with eBay's guidelines and your product category. Clearly communicate your policy in your listings and adhere to it consistently.

- Payment Security: Ensure you offer secure payment options through eBay-approved methods to protect both you and your buyers.
- Comply with eBay Policies: Familiarize yourself with and strictly adhere to eBay's policies regarding prohibited items, listing practices, and seller conduct. This demonstrates your commitment to a safe and fair marketplace.

Going the Extra Mile:

- Offer Guarantees: Consider offering additional guarantees or warranties, if applicable, to showcase your confidence in your products and provide buyer peace of mind.
- Personalized Touches: Add handwritten notes, small gifts, or other gestures of appreciation to personalize the buying experience and leave a lasting positive impression.
- Community Engagement: Participate in relevant eBay forums and discussions to answer questions, share your expertise,

and build relationships with potential buyers.

CHAPTER 4

Finding Treasure in Your Closet: Sourcing Products to Sell

Congratulations on establishing a strong foundation for trust and transparency on eBay! Now it's time to delve into sourcing products – the very lifeblood of your selling journey. This chapter will equip you with valuable strategies for finding hidden treasures in your own closet and beyond, while also helping you identify profitable items to list with confidence.

Treasure Hunting at Home:

- Declutter and Categorize: Start by thoroughly examining your belongings. Categorize items by type, condition, and potential value. Look for vintage clothing, collectibles, electronics, or anything with unique appeal.
- Unearthed Gems: Consider items you no longer use but might hold value for

others, such as childhood toys, inherited items, or unused hobbies.
- **Sentimental Value vs. Selling Potential:** Be mindful of sentimental attachments while evaluating potential profit. Sometimes, letting go can unlock financial opportunities.

Expanding Your Search:

- Garage Sales and Flea Markets: Explore local garage sales, flea markets, and thrift stores for hidden treasures at bargain prices. Hone your negotiation skills and research potential resale value before buying.
- Estate Sales and Auctions: Attend estate sales and online auctions, where you might find unique items at competitive prices. Be prepared to act quickly and strategically.
- Online Marketplaces: Utilize online marketplaces like Facebook Marketplace, Craigslist, or OfferUp to find pre-owned items with potential. Research their selling history on eBay to gauge profitability.

- Wholesalers and Liquidators: Consider sourcing products in bulk from wholesalers or liquidators, offering potential cost savings and wider selection. Research minimum order quantities and profit margins carefully.

Identifying Profitable Items:

- Research, Research, Research: Utilize online tools like Terapeak, Sellbrite, or eBay completed listings to analyze past sales data, identify trending items, and estimate selling prices.
- Consider Seasonality and Trends: Pay attention to seasonal trends and popular niches to predict demand and maximize profit potential.
- Competition and Saturation: Analyze the level of competition for similar items before investing. Oversaturated niches might offer lower profit margins.
- Condition and Value: Prioritize items in good condition with higher perceived value to attract buyers and justify competitive pricing.

- Shipping Costs and Fees: Factor in shipping costs, eBay fees, and potential returns when calculating your final profit margin.

Understanding Market Trends and Researching Your Competition

Now, it's time to master the art of market analysis to optimize your listings and stay ahead of the curve.

Decoding Market Trends:

- Stay Informed: Utilize industry publications, online resources, and eBay seller tools to stay updated on current trends in your niche and broader market.
- Identify Shifting Demands: Analyze search trends, best-selling items, and seasonal fluctuations to understand evolving buyer preferences and adapt your offerings accordingly.
- Emerging Niches: Be on the lookout for emerging niches with growing demand

and less competition, offering an opportunity to establish yourself early.
- Economic Factors: Consider external factors like economic shifts, social media trends, and global events that might impact your target audience's buying behavior.

Competitive Intelligence:

- Identify Direct Competitors: Research sellers who offer similar items in your niche. Analyze their listings, pricing strategies, and marketing tactics.
- Track Their Performance: Monitor their feedback scores, sales volume, and listing trends to understand their strengths and weaknesses.
- Competitive Differentiation: Identify opportunities to differentiate your offerings, such as unique product descriptions, faster shipping, or bundled deals.
- Pricing Benchmarking: Analyze your competitors' pricing to ensure you're offering competitive prices while maintaining healthy profit margins.

Market Research Tools:

- eBay Terapeak: Analyze trends, identify profitable niches, and estimate selling prices based on historical data.
- Sellbrite: Track competitor listings, pricing, and promotions to stay ahead of the curve.
- Social Media Listening Tools: Monitor social media platforms to understand buyer sentiment and emerging trends.
- Industry Publications and Reports:Stay informed about industry news, market forecasts, and expert insights.

Ethical Sourcing

1. Supplier Verification:
   - Thoroughly vet and verify suppliers to ensure they adhere to ethical and sustainable practices. Look for certifications or memberships in recognized industry associations.
2. Transparency in the Supply Chain:

- Prioritize suppliers who maintain transparency in their supply chain. This includes providing information about sourcing, production, and labor practices.
3. Fair Labor Practices:
    - Choose suppliers and manufacturers that adhere to fair labor practices. Ensure workers are treated ethically, paid fairly, and work in safe conditions.
4. Environmental Impact:
    - Consider the environmental impact of your products. Choose suppliers who use sustainable materials, minimize waste, and follow eco-friendly manufacturing processes.
5. Social Responsibility:
    - Support suppliers with strong social responsibility initiatives. This includes contributions to local communities, charitable activities, or partnerships with ethical organizations.
6. Ethical Certifications:

- Look for products with recognized ethical certifications, such as Fair Trade or Ethical Trading Initiative labels. These certifications validate a commitment to ethical sourcing.
7. Continuous Monitoring:
    - Regularly assess and monitor your supply chain for ethical compliance. Maintain an ongoing relationship with suppliers and address any concerns promptly.

Avoiding Restricted Items:

1. Understanding eBay's Restricted Items Policy:
    - Familiarize yourself with eBay's policies on restricted items. Ensure your products comply with these guidelines to avoid account issues and potential legal consequences.
2. Thorough Product Research:
    - Conduct thorough research on each product before listing. Ensure it complies with eBay's policies

and does not fall into any restricted categories.
3. Stay Informed About Legal Regulations:
   - Keep abreast of legal regulations related to your products. Some items may be legal in one region but restricted or prohibited in another. Understand and comply with regional laws.
4. Check Import and Export Regulations:
   - If you source products internationally, be aware of import and export regulations. Some items may be subject to restrictions or require special documentation for cross-border transactions.
5. Consult with Legal Professionals:
   - If uncertain about the legality of a product, consult with legal professionals specializing in e-commerce or product regulations. They can provide specific guidance tailored to your situation.
6. Review eBay's Prohibited and Restricted Items List:

- Regularly review eBay's official list of prohibited and restricted items. This list is updated periodically, and staying informed helps you avoid listing items that could lead to account issues.
7. Carefully Check Product Descriptions:
    - Carefully read and understand product descriptions. Some seemingly innocent items may have components or uses that make them restricted.
8. Customer Feedback and Inquiries:
    - Pay attention to customer feedback and inquiries about your products. Address any concerns promptly and consider discontinuing items that raise ethical or legal issues.

eBay Restricted Items Policy Overview

eBay has strict policies regarding the sale of certain items to ensure a safe and compliant marketplace. The list of restricted items includes, but is not limited to:

1. Illegal Items: Items that are prohibited by law or regulation, including stolen property, illegal drugs, and items subject to export restrictions.
2. Hazardous Materials: Products that pose a safety risk, such as explosives, fireworks, and certain chemicals.
3. Counterfeit Items: Sale of counterfeit or replica items is strictly prohibited.
4. Weapons: Firearms, ammunition, and certain accessories may be restricted or prohibited.
5. Human Parts and Remains: The sale of human body parts, organs, and remains is not allowed.
6. Animal Products: Certain animal products, such as ivory and items made from endangered species, may be restricted.

7. Government and Transit-Related Items: Items related to law enforcement, government, and public transit may have restrictions.
8. Drugs and Drug Paraphernalia: Prescription drugs, illegal drugs, and related paraphernalia are prohibited.
9. Adult Content: Explicit adult content and certain adult items are restricted.
10. Prohibited Services: Certain services, such as hacking services and academic writing services, are not allowed.

CHAPTER 5

Crafting Listings that Convert

Crafting listings that convert on eBay involves a strategic and compelling approach to showcase your products. Start with a captivating title that incorporates relevant keywords, highlights key features, and adds a unique selling proposition. For example, a title like "Premium Wireless Noise-Canceling Headphones - Immerse Yourself in Crystal Clear Sound!" can capture attention. Include high-quality images that provide a clear view of your product from various angles, utilizing good lighting to highlight any unique details. Your description should be detailed yet concise, covering features, specifications, and benefits while maintaining honesty about any imperfections. Organize information with bullet points for easy scanning, and integrate keywords naturally throughout the description.

Pricing strategy is crucial, so consider offering competitive prices, discounts, or promotions to attract potential buyers. Clearly communicate any special pricing within your listing. Showcase the unique selling points of your product, whether it's exclusive features, a special edition, or unique benefits, to differentiate your listing. Incorporating limited-time offers or promotions creates a sense of urgency, encouraging buyers to act quickly. Clearly outline shipping information, including policies and estimated delivery times, and offer expedited shipping options if possible.

Ensure your listing is mobile-friendly for the growing number of buyers who use smartphones for browsing and purchasing. Include trust-building elements such as your seller ratings, positive feedback, and clear return policies to instill confidence in potential buyers. End your listing with a strong call-to-action, reinforcing the value of your product and encouraging buyers to make a purchase. Additionally, emphasize your commitment to excellent customer service by promptly responding to inquiries, addressing concerns, and providing assistance throughout the purchasing process. Experiment with A/B testing to optimize different elements of your listings based on performance and customer feedback. Continuous improvement and adaptation are essential for crafting listings that not only attract attention but also convert browsers into satisfied buyers.

Writing Eye-Catching Titles

1. Keyword Optimization:
    - Include relevant keywords in your title to enhance search visibility. Consider what potential buyers might search for when looking for your item.
2. Clear and Concise Language:
    - Keep titles concise while conveying essential information. Avoid unnecessary words and focus on key details that make your item stand out.
3. Highlight Key Features:
    - Highlight unique or standout features of your item in the title. What makes it special? Communicate this upfront to capture buyer attention.
4. Use Capitals and Punctuation Wisely:

- Capitalize the first letter of each major word for readability. Use punctuation sparingly but effectively to create a polished look.
5. Invoke a Sense of Urgency or Scarcity:
    - If applicable, create a sense of urgency or scarcity in the title. Words like "limited edition" or "last chance" can encourage quicker buyer engagement.
6. Price Inclusion (if Competitive):
    - Consider including your competitive pricing in the title if it's a strong selling point. However, this is optional and may not be suitable for all items.
7. Brand Mention (if Recognizable):
    - Include the brand name if it's well-known and adds value to your item. Buyers often search for specific brands when looking for certain products.
8. Avoid All Caps:
    - Avoid using all capital letters as it can be perceived as shouting and is against eBay's guidelines. Opt

for a balanced mix of uppercase and lowercase letters.
9. Check Spelling and Grammar:
    - Ensure your title is free of spelling and grammar errors. A well-written title contributes to a professional appearance.

Writing Detailed Descriptions

1. Start with a Hook:
    - Begin your description with an engaging hook that captures the buyer's interest. This can be a benefit, a unique feature, or a solution your product provides.
2. Provide Comprehensive Details:
    - Include all relevant details about your item, such as size, color, dimensions, and condition. The goal is to answer potential questions preemptively.
3. Be Honest and Transparent:
    - Transparency builds trust. Clearly mention any flaws or imperfections in the item. Buyers

appreciate honesty, and it can help avoid issues later.
4. Use Bullet Points for Readability:
    - Organize information using bullet points for easy readability. This format makes it simpler for buyers to scan and absorb key details.
5. Tell a Story (if Applicable):
    - If your item has a unique backstory or history, consider incorporating it into the description. Storytelling can create a connection with buyers.
6. Highlight Benefits:
    - Clearly outline the benefits of your product. How will it improve the buyer's life? Emphasize these points throughout your description.
7. Include Usage Instructions (if Relevant):
    - If your item requires specific instructions for use, maintenance, or assembly, provide clear and concise guidelines in your description.
8. Encourage Questions:

- Invite buyers to ask questions if they have any uncertainties. This shows that you are open to communication and willing to provide additional information.
9. Mobile-Friendly Formatting:
    - Ensure your description is easy to read on mobile devices. Many buyers browse and make purchases using smartphones, so mobile-friendly formatting is essential.
10. End with a Call-to-Action:
    - Conclude your description with a clear call-to-action. Encourage buyers to make a purchase, ask questions, or explore related items in your store.

Let's go through an example of writing an eye-catching title and a detailed description for a fictional item, a vintage camera.

Eye-Catching Title:

Capture Timeless Moments with Vintage Kodak Film Camera - Limited Edition!

In this example, we've included keywords like "vintage," "Kodak," and "film camera" to enhance search visibility. The addition of "Limited Edition" creates a sense of exclusivity and urgency, encouraging potential buyers to take a closer look.

Detailed Description:

Unleash your inner photographer with this exquisite Vintage Kodak Film Camera – a true gem for photography enthusiasts and collectors alike. This limited edition piece not only captures timeless moments but also transports you back to the golden age of analog photography.

Key Features:

- Classic Design: Embrace the aesthetics of a bygone era with the camera's classic and elegant design.

- Fully Functional: Despite its vintage charm, this Kodak camera is fully functional, ready to bring your creative vision to life.
- Rich Film Experience: Rediscover the joy of shooting on film, immersing yourself in the unique and authentic photographic experience.

Details:

This camera boasts a pristine exterior and is free from any scratches or dents. The lens is crystal clear, ensuring crisp and vibrant images. The vintage leather case, included with the camera, adds to its allure and provides protection.

Condition: Excellent vintage condition, with no signs of wear. The camera has been well-maintained and is in perfect working order.

Specifications:

- Brand: Kodak
- Model: [Model Name]

- Film Type: 35mm
- Year of Manufacture: [Year]
- Accessories: Original leather case

Story Behind the Camera:

This camera holds a special place in the history of photography, having been part of a renowned photographer's collection. Its journey includes capturing memorable moments, and now, it's ready to embark on a new chapter with you.

Your Purchase Includes:

- Vintage Kodak Film Camera
- Original Leather Case
- [Any additional items]

Don't miss the opportunity to own this limited edition vintage camera and add a touch of nostalgia to your photography collection. Embrace the art of analog photography and let this Kodak camera be your companion in creating enduring memories. Feel free to reach out with any questions or for more details. Happy shooting!

In this detailed description, we've provided comprehensive information about the camera, highlighted key features, shared its story, and invited potential buyers to engage with questions. This approach aims to create a connection with the buyer and communicate the unique value of the item.

Optimizing for Search with Keyword Research

To optimize your eBay listings for search, it's crucial to conduct effective keyword research. Begin by gaining a comprehensive understanding of your product, identifying its main features, specifications, and potential use cases. Brainstorm relevant terms and leverage eBay's search bar to explore popular and related keywords, using its autofill suggestions for insights. Analyze competitor listings to identify successful keywords in your niche and utilize eBay's listing analytics to understand which terms are driving traffic to your items.

Incorporate a mix of generic and specific keywords, including long-tail phrases to target a niche audience. Utilize eBay's item specifics fields when creating your listings, as eBay often relies on this information to improve search results. Think like a buyer, considering the language they might use in searches, and be mindful of seasonal keywords if applicable. Regularly monitor the performance of your listings through eBay's analytics and adjust your keyword strategy based on insights.

For instance, if you're selling a Nikon DSLR camera, include keywords like "digital camera," "Nikon DSLR," "20MP camera," "photography equipment," and specific model names such as "Nikon D750." Remember to align your chosen keywords with eBay's policies to avoid any penalties. By strategically incorporating researched keywords into your listings, you enhance their visibility, increasing the likelihood of attracting relevant buyers to your eBay store. Stay proactive in reassessing and adjusting your keyword strategy based on the performance of your listings and changes in market trends.

Using High-Quality Pictures and Videos to Showcase Your Products

Taking awesome pictures of your crafts is super important when you're selling stuff online, especially on places like eBay. Think of your photos as your items' online faces – if they look meh, your things won't sell well. It's as straightforward as that. Even if you're a wizard at making cool stuff, no one will notice if your pictures aren't clear and nice.

Big stores can afford fancy photographers to make their things look amazing online because they're selling tons of each item. But for smaller handmade businesses, like yours, getting a professional photographer for every little thing is way too pricey. So, you've got to learn how to take awesome pics yourself. Good news, though – with today's cool cameras and lots of examples from other crafty people online, you can totally learn to take your own great product photos.

A top-notch product photo is one that's really clear and sharp. When someone looks at it, they should be able to see all the little details, textures, and how awesome your item is. It's like telling a story about your creation through pictures. Lighting is key – a well-lit photo shows off the true colors of your product. That's crucial because your photos need to show exactly what your buyer will get.

Meet Jake, for example. He takes good photos of his hand-carved wooden spoons. He makes sure to use good lighting and takes pics from different angles to show off all the cool details. No fancy camera tricks – just clear and bright photos.

In the world of selling stuff online, your photos are your secret weapon. If you can make your crafts look amazing in pictures, you'll attract more buyers. So, grab your camera, find some good light, and let your creations shine online, especially on places like eBay!

Smooth lighting without strong flash shadows or blinding reflections from direct spotlights is essential for a successful product photo. It all comes down to having light that is both bright and soft; the secret is to become proficient with reflected or diffused light.

Excellent product photography focuses on the finer points. Close-up photos highlight the artistry of a handmade object, such as the rich texture of handwoven fabric, the detailed stitching on a fabric tote, or the distinctive clasps on a beaded necklace.

A well-taken product photo sets the item against a plain background that enhances rather than detracts from the goods. The background should highlight the object so that it becomes the focal point of the image, not take away from it. A traditional option is a white background with soft shadows. While black velvet might add a touch of elegance when presenting jewelry in person, it doesn't translate well for product photos. Opt for lighter backgrounds to enhance your product's visibility and overall appeal. Natural walls in beige or brown, stone, and worn wood are also excellent settings for handcrafted objects.

Your photos should go beyond mere product display; they should convey the versatility of your item and the varied needs it fulfills. Suppose your product is a popular home decor item – showcase it in a setting that highlights its aesthetic appeal.

Incorporate at least one image featuring a model where relevant. If you craft unique hand-painted vases, show one on a table, but the photo of the vase adorning a chic living room adds a personalized touch. Display bracelets on elegant wrists, wrap scarves around shoulders, and position hats on stylish heads. Notice how the expressions and postures of models contribute to setting the tone for an item – the human element captures attention.

For some one-of-a-kind items, it might be best not to showcase them on a model. Some buyers prefer the assurance that the item they're eyeing hasn't been worn by someone else. Instead, photograph earrings hanging from a branch or displayed creatively, avoiding direct contact with a model. If you capture a model using your intricately designed home decor, explicitly mention in the description that the item shipped will be brand new.

Invest time in preparing and arranging products meticulously to capture the best images. Smooth out wrinkles on fabrics, arrange fiber items neatly, polish ceramics, and showcase finished woodwork in its best light. Craft visually appealing arrangements – consider it your creative stage! Arrange that handmade quilt in a cozy setting to showcase its warmth, create an artful display of pottery, stack bowls in a vibrant formation, or hang uniquely designed handbags on a decorative rack. A stellar product photo not only highlights your item but also communicates the care and attention to detail you put into your craft from start to finish.

How to take a good product photos

Taking great product photos doesn't require you to be a photography expert. With a few simple steps, you can capture appealing images that showcase your items beautifully. Here's a beginner-friendly guide:

1. Seek Inspiration Online:
    - Before diving into photography, check out similar products online. Look for successful listings on platforms like eBay to get an idea of how products are showcased. This can inspire your own creative approach.

2. Camera Considerations:
    - While you don't need a top-of-the-line camera, investing in a decent one can significantly enhance your photos. Consider a point-and-shoot camera or even a smartphone with a good camera. Smartphones like the iPhone or Samsung Galaxy series often have excellent built-in cameras.
3. What to Consider Before Buying a Camera:
    - If you decide to invest in a camera, consider factors like megapixels (for image clarity), autofocus capabilities, and ease of use. Look for a camera that suits your needs without overwhelming you with complex settings. Entry-level DSLRs or mirrorless cameras are great choices for beginners.
4. Power and Focus:
    - Ensure that your camera has sufficient power, whether it's a rechargeable battery or standard batteries. A good autofocus feature is crucial, especially when

capturing details. This ensures your product is sharp and clear in the photos.
5. Mastering Lighting:
    - Lighting is key to a fantastic product photo. Natural light is often the best, so try to take your photos near a window during the day. If shooting indoors, use soft, diffused lighting to avoid harsh shadows. Avoid relying solely on overhead lights or direct sunlight.
6. Setting the Scene:
    - Choose a clean and uncluttered background to let your product shine. A white or neutral background is classic and ensures your item is the focal point. Experiment with different angles and compositions to find what works best for your product.
7. Composition Tips:
    - Place your product front and center, ensuring it fills the frame. Experiment with close-up shots to highlight details. Use props

sparingly to enhance your product without overshadowing it.
8. Editing:
    - After taking your photos, consider simple editing to enhance colors or correct exposure. Many smartphones have built-in editing tools, or you can use free online tools like Canva or Adobe Spark.

Online Photo Editing Tools

- Adobe Spark
- Canva
- Pixlr
- Fotor
- PicMonkey

Downloadable Photo Editing Software:

1. Adobe Photoshop
2. GIMP (GNU Image Manipulation Program)
3. Lightroom
4. Capture One
5. Affinity Photo

These tools vary in complexity and features, so you can choose the one that best suits your needs and comfort level with photo editing. Whether you opt for online tools or downloadable software, these resources provide a range of options to enhance and refine your product photos.

CHAPTER 6

Pricing to Win: Profitable Strategies for Beginners

Setting the right prices is a critical aspect of success on eBay, especially for beginners navigating the online marketplace. A key strategy is to thoroughly research competitors, understanding market dynamics, and analyzing successful sellers' pricing approaches. Starting with competitive prices can be advantageous as it attracts initial buyers, helping build a positive reputation and visibility. Considering options like offering free shipping, creating bundle deals, and using dynamic pricing strategies keeps your approach flexible. Utilize auctions for unique items and employ "Buy It Now" for more common products, providing stability in pricing. Offering additional value through excellent services and periodic promotions or discounts can enhance your listings. Building trust with competitive prices and consistently delivering value will likely encourage repeat business. Regularly monitor and analyze your sales data, allowing you to refine and optimize your pricing strategy based on market trends, demand, and competition. Adaptability and a willingness to learn from your selling experiences will contribute to your overall success on eBay.

Understanding Fees and Calculating Your Bottom Line

Understanding the fees associated with selling on eBay is crucial for calculating your bottom line. Familiarize yourself with insertion fees, final value fees, and any additional charges. Consider how these fees impact your overall profit margins when setting prices for your items.

Let's delve deeper into the fees associated with selling on eBay:

1. Insertion Fees:
    - Insertion fees are charges incurred for listing an item on eBay. Typically, sellers receive a certain number of free listings each month, but exceeding that limit incurs a fee. The fee varies based on the item's category and the

listing format (auction-style or fixed price).
2. Final Value Fees:
    - Final value fees are a percentage of the total sale amount, including shipping costs. This fee is charged when an item is sold. The percentage depends on the item category, and additional fees may apply for optional listing upgrades.
3. Additional Fees:
    - eBay may charge additional fees for optional services or features, such as promoting your listing, using advanced listing tools, or offering certain shipping services. It's essential to understand these optional fees and evaluate whether they align with your selling strategy.
4. Payment Processing Fees:
    - If you use eBay's managed payments, you'll encounter payment processing fees. These fees cover the cost of processing transactions and depend on the

payment method used by the buyer.
5. Subscription Fees:
    - eBay offers subscription plans, like the eBay Store subscription, which provides various benefits, including discounted fees and additional free listings. Sellers need to evaluate whether a subscription plan aligns with their selling volume and goals.
6. International Fees:
    - Selling internationally may incur additional fees, such as international shipping fees and currency conversion fees. Be aware of these costs when deciding to offer your products globally.
7. Returns and Refunds:
    - While not a direct fee, managing returns and refunds can impact your bottom line. Factor in potential return shipping costs and consider eBay's policies regarding return-related fees.

Calculating Your Bottom Line

The "bottom line" in business refers to the net profit or loss after accounting for all expenses, costs, and revenue. It represents the financial result of a business's operations. To calculate the bottom line for an individual sale or overall business performance, you can use the following formula:

Bottom Line=Total Revenue−Total Costs

Bottom Line=Total Revenue−Total Costs

In the context of selling on eBay, the bottom line for a specific sale would be the profit from that transaction, considering all associated costs and fees. Here's a simplified version:

Profit=Total Revenue−Total Costs (including eBay fees, shipping costs, product costs, etc.)

It's important to include all relevant costs associated with the sale, such as the cost of the item, eBay fees (insertion fees, final value fees), shipping costs, packaging costs, and any other expenses incurred in the process.

By accurately calculating the bottom line for each sale, you gain insights into the profitability of your transactions and can make informed decisions about pricing, costs, and overall business strategy.

Setting Competitive Prices with Auction Formats or Buy It Now

Choosing the right pricing strategy and format for your eBay listings is crucial for attracting buyers and maximizing profits. This guide delves into setting competitive prices for both auction and Buy It Now formats, equipping you with the knowledge and tools to make informed decisions and achieve success on the eBay marketplace.

Understanding the Formats:

- Auction Format: Buyers compete through bidding, driving the price up until the auction ends. Ideal for unique,

rare, or high-demand items where competition can inflate the price.
- Buy It Now Format: Set a fixed price for immediate purchase. Offers convenience and predictability for buyers, but requires careful pricing to be competitive.

Competitive Pricing Strategies:

Auction Format:

- Starting Price:
    - Research: Analyze similar past auctions to understand typical starting and ending prices.
    - Attract Bids: Start slightly lower to encourage initial bids and build momentum.
    - Reserve Price (Optional): Set a minimum acceptable price to avoid selling below value.
    -
- Reserve Price Strategy:
    - No Reserve: Encourages aggressive bidding but carries the risk of selling below expectations.

- - Hidden Reserve: Buyers unaware of the reserve, creating excitement while protecting your minimum price.

- Ending Time:
  - Peak Traffic Days/Times: Schedule auctions to end during times with high buyer activity.
  - Extended Listings: Consider longer durations for valuable items or to attract more bids.

Buy It Now Format:

- Competitive Analysis: Research similar Buy It Now listings, considering their price, condition, and selling history.
- Psychological Pricing: Experiment with price points ending in ".99" or strategic anchoring (starting slightly higher with potential discounts).
- Value-Added Services: Factor in the cost of free shipping, returns, or other services when setting your price.

- Promotional Strategies: Offer limited-time discounts, bundles, or sales to attract buyers.

Choosing the Right Format:

- Consider the Item:
    - Unique/Rare: Auctions might generate higher prices due to bidding competition.
    - Common/Readily Available: Buy It Now offers convenience and faster sales.
    -
- Your Time Commitment:
    - Auctions: Require managing bids, answering questions, and monitoring the ending.
    - Buy It Now: Less active management but requires accurate upfront pricing.
    -
- Risk Tolerance:
    - Auctions: Potential for selling below your desired price.

- Buy It Now: Fixed price offers certainty but might require lower pricing to be competitive.

Promotions and Discounts to Attract Buyers and Boost Sales

The Power of Promotions:

- Attract New Buyers: Entice potential buyers with deals they can't resist, expanding your customer base.
- Boost Sales Velocity: Move inventory faster, freeing up cash flow and generating capital for reinvestment.
- Clear Out Slow-Moving Stock: Generate interest in older, stagnant items with strategic discounts.
- Reward Loyal Customers: Show appreciation and encourage repeat business with exclusive offers.
- Create a Sense of Urgency: Limited-time deals encourage impulsive purchases and capitalize on buyer FOMO (fear of missing out).

Types of Promotions:

- Percentage Discounts: Offer a flat discount off the listed price, clearly stating the percentage saved.
- Fixed Amount Discounts: Reduce the price by a specific dollar amount, highlighting the actual price reduction.
- Buy One, Get One (BOGO) Deals: Offer a free or discounted item with the purchase of another, encouraging higher order values.
- Bundles and Multi-Item Discounts: Group complementary items at a discounted price, promoting higher average order values.
- Free Shipping Promotions: Offer free shipping to incentivize purchases, especially for higher-priced items.
- Limited-Time Sales: Create a sense of urgency with flash sales, weekend deals, or holiday promotions.
- Coupons and Vouchers: Distribute codes for specific discounts, attracting new buyers or rewarding loyal customers.

Crafting Effective Promotions:

- Target the Right Audience: Tailor your promotions to specific buyer segments based on their preferences and purchase history.
- Clearly Communicate the Offer: Ensure your promotion's terms and conditions are easy to understand, avoiding confusion.
- Highlight the Value Proposition: Emphasize the benefits buyers get, focusing on savings, convenience, or added value.
- Promote Effectively: Utilize eBay's promotional tools, social media channels, and email marketing to reach your target audience.
- Track and Analyze Results: Monitor the performance of your promotions to understand their impact on sales, conversion rates, and customer engagement.

Creative Discount Ideas:

- Secret Sale Codes: Offer exclusive discounts to email subscribers or social media followers.

- Milestone Discounts: Celebrate reaching a sales goal with a storewide discount.
- Referral Rewards: incentivize existing customers to refer new buyers with discounts or special offers.
- Mystery Boxes: Create curated bundles with surprise items at a discounted price, adding an element of fun and excitement.
- Gamification: Implement point systems or challenges with discount rewards to boost engagement.

Remember: Promotions are strategic tools, not magic solutions. Use them thoughtfully, analyze their impact, and continuously refine your approach to maximize their effectiveness in attracting buyers, boosting sales, and achieving your eBay goals.

CHAPTER 7

Shipping and Delivery Made Easy

Choosing the Right Methods and Costs

As you embark on your eBay selling journey, navigating the complexities of shipping methods and costs can seem daunting. But fear not! This comprehensive guide equips you with the knowledge and tools to make informed decisions, ensuring satisfied customers, efficient deliveries, and profitable sales.

Understanding Your Options:

The world of eBay shipping offers a diverse range of methods, each with its own unique characteristics:

- Ground Shipping: Cost-effective for heavier items or longer distances, with options like standard ground, expedited ground, and media mail.

- Air Shipping: Faster delivery for time-sensitive items, but comes with a higher price tag. Options include priority mail, priority mail express, and international shipping.
- Calculated Shipping: eBay automatically calculates costs based on buyer location, package weight, and dimensions.
- Flat Rate Shipping: Offer a fixed shipping price regardless of buyer location, ideal for lightweight items or standardized packaging.
- Free Shipping: Entice buyers by absorbing shipping costs yourself, factoring it into your pricing strategy.

Choosing the Right Method:

The optimal shipping method depends on several factors:

- Item Value and Weight: Consider the cost versus value of your item. Fragile or valuable items might warrant faster, more secure shipping.
- Customer Expectations: Understand your target audience's typical shipping

preferences. Balancing speed and affordability is key.
- Profit Margin: Ensure your chosen method doesn't eat into your profits. Calculate shipping costs into your pricing strategy.
- Delivery Timeframe: Offer options that cater to different needs, from express delivery for urgent purchases to budget-friendly slower options.

Cost Considerations:

- Compare Rates: Utilize eBay's shipping calculator and compare rates from different carriers to find the most cost-effective option.
- Packaging Costs: Factor in the cost of packaging materials like boxes, tape, and cushioning to ensure safe and secure delivery.
- Handling Fees: Be aware of any additional handling fees charged by eBay or shipping carriers.

Offering Competitive Shipping:

- Free Shipping Incentives: Strategically offer free shipping on specific items or purchases above a certain amount to attract buyers.
- Combined Shipping Discounts: Encourage multi-item purchases by offering combined shipping discounts for items bought together.
- Clear Communication: Communicate shipping costs transparently in your listings to avoid buyer confusion and dissatisfaction.

Additional Tips:

- Choose Reliable Carriers: Opt for reputable carriers with good track records for on-time deliveries and minimal damage.
- Offer Tracking: Provide buyers with tracking information to enhance transparency and build trust.

Packaging Your Products for Safe and Happy Deliveries

As an eBay seller, ensuring your products arrive at their destination safe and sound is paramount. Not only does it prevent damage and unhappy customers, but it also reflects your professionalism and commitment to quality. This guide equips you with the knowledge and techniques to package your products effectively, ensuring smooth deliveries and satisfied buyers.

Understanding Your Packaging Needs:

- Product Fragility: Delicate items require extra care with cushioning and sturdy boxes.
- Item Size and Shape: Choose appropriate box sizes to prevent movement and potential damage.
- Shipping Distance: Longer journeys might necessitate reinforced packaging for added protection.
- Weather Conditions: Consider potential rain, snow, or heat and choose packaging materials accordingly.

Packaging Essentials:

- Corrugated Cardboard Boxes: Opt for sturdy, double-walled boxes to withstand handling and transportation.
- Packing Peanuts or Bubble Wrap: Provide cushioning and absorb impact, especially for fragile items.
- Void Fillers: Utilize crumpled paper, air pillows, or other materials to fill empty spaces and prevent shifting.
- Packing Tape: Secure boxes tightly with strong packing tape to ensure closure and prevent tampering.
- Shipping Labels: Clearly print and affix shipping labels with accurate recipient information and tracking details.

Packing Techniques:

- Inner Wrapping: Wrap fragile items individually with bubble wrap or tissue paper for added protection.
- Secure Cushioning: Use sufficient cushioning material to prevent items from moving within the box.

- Box Filling: Fill any empty space with void fillers to prevent items from shifting during transit.
- Sealing: Secure the box tightly with packing tape, applying multiple strips for reinforcement.
- Labeling: Clearly and securely affix shipping labels on a flat surface of the box.

Additional Tips:

- Oversized Items: Consider using wooden crates for large or irregularly shaped items to ensure stability.
- Double Boxing: For valuable or fragile items, nest a smaller box inside a larger one with additional cushioning.
- Special Considerations: Research specific packaging requirements for hazardous materials or items with temperature sensitivity.
- Recycle and Reuse: Whenever possible, opt for eco-friendly packaging materials and reuse boxes in good condition.
- Invest in Quality: Don't skimp on packaging materials, as proper

protection can prevent costly damage claims and negative feedback.

A Guide to International Shipping on eBay

Expanding your eBay reach to international buyers unlocks exciting opportunities. But navigating the complexities of international shipping, customs, and regulations can seem daunting. Fear not, intrepid seller! This guide equips you with the knowledge and strategies to overcome these hurdles and successfully ship your products across borders.

Understanding the Landscape:

- Customs and Duties: Each country has its own customs regulations and import duties. Familiarize yourself with the requirements for your target markets.
- Documentation: Prepare necessary customs forms and invoices accurately, including item descriptions, values, and HS codes (Harmonized System codes).

- Prohibited Items: Be aware of items restricted or prohibited in certain countries to avoid shipment delays or seizures.
- Shipping Restrictions: Certain carriers might have limitations on specific items or destinations. Research thoroughly before choosing a carrier.

International Shipping Methods:

- eBay International Standard Delivery: A convenient program handling international shipping and customs for eligible US sellers.
- Calculated Shipping: eBay automatically calculates costs based on weight, dimensions, and destination.
- Flat Rate Shipping: Offer a fixed price for international shipping, potentially attracting budget-conscious buyers.
- International Priority Shipping: Faster delivery options like airmail or express services come at a higher cost.

Customs Clearance and Duties:

- Incoterms: Understand trade terms like Delivered Duty Paid (DDP) or Ex Works (EXW) to clarify who is responsible for customs duties.
- Prepaid Duties: Consider offering to prepay customs duties for a smoother buying experience, potentially factoring it into your pricing.
- Transparency: Clearly communicate potential customs charges to buyers to avoid surprises and dissatisfaction.

CHAPTER 8

Customer Service 101 (Building Trust and Handling Inquiries)

Effective communication is essential for eBay sellers to establish a positive reputation and build trust with buyers. Prompt responses and a professional tone play a crucial role in creating a satisfactory experience for customers.

The Power of Prompt Responses:

- Build Trust and Confidence: Timely replies demonstrate your professionalism and commitment to customer satisfaction.
- Reduce Buyer Anxiety: Prompt responses address concerns quickly, preventing frustration and potential negative feedback.
- Increase Sales Opportunities: By being readily available, you can answer questions, clarify details, and convert hesitant buyers into satisfied customers.
- Boost Your eBay Star Rating: Consistent promptness contributes to positive

feedback, improving your seller reputation and visibility.

Strategies for Speedy Replies:

- Set Expectations: Clearly communicate your typical response time in your listings and profile.
- Utilize Mobile Notifications: Enable notifications on your phone or tablet to stay informed of buyer messages.
- Schedule Response Time: Set aside dedicated times daily to respond to messages promptly.
- Prioritize Urgent Inquiries: Address questions about bids, purchases, or potential issues first.
- Utilize Canned Responses: Create pre-written templates for frequently asked questions to save time while maintaining personalization.

Maintaining a Professional Tone:

- Courtesy and Respect: Treat all buyers with respect, even in challenging situations.

- Clear and Concise Communication: Communicate clearly and avoid jargon to ensure understanding.
- Proofread Before Sending: Double-check messages for typos and grammatical errors to maintain professionalism.
- Positive and Solution-Oriented: Focus on resolving issues promptly and efficiently, maintaining a positive attitude.
- Avoid Emotional Responses: Stay professional and avoid getting into emotional exchanges with buyers, even if they are upset.

Addressing Buyer Concerns and Handling Disputes

Addressing buyer concerns and effectively handling disputes is crucial for eBay sellers to maintain positive customer relationships and resolve any issues that may arise during a transaction. In this detailed guide, we will provide step-by-step instructions on how to address buyer concerns and handle disputes, along with examples to illustrate each step.

Step 1: Acknowledge the Concern

when a buyer raises a concern or opens a dispute, it is important to acknowledge their issue promptly and let them know that you are taking their concerns seriously. Here's an example of how to acknowledge a concern:

"Dear [Buyer's Name],

Thank you for bringing this matter to our attention. We apologize for any inconvenience you may have experienced and assure you that we are actively working to resolve this issue for you.

Best regards,
[Your Name]"

Step 2: Gather Information and Communicate

To effectively handle a buyer's concern or dispute, gather all relevant information to understand the situation fully. Communicate with the buyer to obtain additional details and provide any necessary information. For example:

"Dear [Buyer's Name],

We appreciate your contacting us regarding the issue you have encountered. In order to assist you better, could you please provide us with more details about the problem? This will help us investigate and resolve the matter quickly.

Additionally, we would like to provide you with some information that might be helpful in resolving the issue."

Step 3: Offer a Solution

once you have gathered all the necessary information, propose a solution to the buyer's concern or dispute. Be flexible and offer options whenever possible to meet the buyer's needs. Here's an example:

"*Dear [Buyer's Name],*

Based on the information you have provided, we understand the inconvenience caused and would like to offer a solution to address the issue. We can either provide a full refund or offer a replacement for the item. Please let us know your preferred option and we will proceed accordingly."

Step 4: Find a Common Ground
In some cases, the buyer's expectation may not align with what can reasonably be offered. In such instances, try to find a common ground that satisfies both parties. This could involve suggesting alternatives or offering additional compensation. For example:

"Dear [Buyer's Name],

We understand your frustration and apologize for any inconvenience caused. Unfortunately, we are unable to offer a full refund in this situation due to the circumstances. However, we would be happy to offer you a partial refund of [amount] or provide you with [additional compensation] as a gesture of goodwill. We believe this fair resolution will help address your concerns effectively."

Step 5: Document everything
throughout the process of addressing a buyer's concern or handling a dispute, it is crucial to maintain a record of all communication and actions taken. Documenting everything helps to have a clear timeline and reference for future reference, if needed.

Step 6: Escalate to eBay Resolution Center, if Necessary

If you are unable to come to a mutually satisfactory resolution with the buyer, you may need to escalate the case to the eBay Resolution Center. eBay can provide arbitration and mediation services to help resolve disputes between buyers and sellers.

Step 7: Stay Professional and Remain Composed

Regardless of the situation, it is important to remain professional and composed throughout the process. Use polite language, be patient, and avoid becoming defensive or confrontational. Remember that resolving the buyer's concern is in the best interest of your reputation as an eBay seller.

By following these steps and addressing buyer concerns with a proactive and customer-oriented approach, you can effectively handle disputes and maintain positive customer relationships on eBay.

Building Repeat Customers and Cultivating Positive Relationships

Building repeat customers and cultivating positive relationships is key to long-term success on eBay. Provide excellent customer service from the beginning by delivering products promptly and as described. Ensure that your items are well-packaged to create a positive unboxing experience.

Encourage repeat business by offering discounts or exclusive promotions for returning customers. Utilize eBay's marketing tools to send personalized offers and messages. Consider creating a loyalty program or providing incentives for customers who make multiple purchases.

Maintain a professional and friendly tone in all communications. Respond promptly to messages, address any issues with empathy, and express gratitude for their business. Positive interactions contribute to a favorable seller rating and encourage buyers to return.

Regularly update your inventory with new and exciting items. Consider reaching out to previous customers with notifications about your latest listings. Building a connection with your customers goes beyond the transaction; it involves creating a memorable and positive experience that encourages loyalty.

By consistently providing great products and exceptional customer service, you can create a loyal customer base that not only returns for future purchases but also recommends your eBay store to others. Cultivating positive relationships is an investment in the long-term success and sustainability of your eBay selling venture.

CHAPTER 9

Tools and Technology to Simplify Your Sales Journey

Inventory Management and Listing Automation for Efficiency

Inventory management refers to the planning, organizing, and controlling of all goods and materials used in a business.

Listing automation involves using tools and software to automate the process of creating and managing product listings on online marketplaces like eBay.

Efficient inventory management and listing automation are essential for eBay sellers to streamline their operations and save time. Proper inventory management ensures that you have accurate stock levels, avoid overselling or running out of stock, and enables you to efficiently fulfill orders. Listing automation helps automate the process of creating and managing listings, saving you time and ensuring consistency. Here are some strategies to achieve efficiency in inventory management and listing automation on eBay:

1. Centralize Inventory Tracking: Use an inventory management system or software to centralize and track your inventory across multiple channels, including eBay. This allows you to have a real-time view of your stock levels, avoid overselling, and streamline the order fulfillment process.
2. Set Reorder Points and Restocking Procedures: Determine reorder points for each product to ensure that you restock before running out of stock. Establish standard procedures for restocking, such as placing orders with suppliers or updating stock quantities when new inventory arrives.
3. Utilize Barcodes or SKUs: Assign unique barcodes or SKUs to each product to facilitate efficient inventory tracking. Barcodes or SKUs enable you to quickly identify and locate products and streamline the order fulfillment process.
4. Implement Batch Listing: Use listing automation tools or software to create and manage listings in bulk. This saves

time compared to creating individual listings manually. You can enter product information, pricing, and quantities in a spreadsheet or CSV file and then upload it to create multiple listings simultaneously.

5. Use Listing Templates: Create listing templates to standardize the format and information included in your listings. This ensures consistency across your listings and saves time when creating new listings.

6. Optimize Product Descriptions and Images: Create comprehensive and accurate product descriptions with relevant keywords to improve search visibility. Use high-quality images that showcase your products from different angles. Investing time in optimizing your listings upfront can generate long-term efficiency and attract more buyers.

7. Schedule Listings: Use eBay's scheduling feature or listing automation software to schedule your listings in advance. This allows you to plan and optimize your listing activity, ensuring a

consistent presence and avoiding any manual listing tasks during peak times.
8. Implement Listing Rules and Policies: Set up listing rules or policies within listing automation tools to ensure compliance with eBay's guidelines. This includes specifying return policies, shipping methods, and any other relevant listing requirements. Automating listing rules eliminates the need for repetitive manual adjustments.
9. Monitor and Update Stock Levels: Regularly review and update your inventory levels to reflect accurate stock availability. This includes updating quantities after sales, returns, or restocking. Automating stock level updates can save time and reduce the risk of overselling.
10. Analyze Sales Data and Optimize Inventory: Use sales data and analytics to identify your top-selling products, slow-moving items, and trends. Based on this information, adjust your inventory levels accordingly to optimize sales and reduce storage costs.

By implementing efficient inventory management practices and leveraging listing automation tools, you can significantly streamline your eBay selling operations and increase productivity. Regularly review and fine-tune your processes to ensure continued efficiency and adaptability to evolving marketplace needs.

Marketing Strategies:

- eBay Promoted Listings: Advertise your listings within eBay search results and gain valuable visibility.
- Social Media Marketing: Leverage platforms like Facebook, Instagram, and Twitter to showcase products and connect with potential buyers.
- Content Marketing: Create informative and engaging blog posts, articles, or videos related to your products and niche.
- Email Marketing: Build an email list and send targeted campaigns with promotions, new product announcements, and special offers.

- Influencer Marketing: Partner with relevant influencers in your niche to reach a wider audience and build trust.

Promotional Strategies:

- Discounts and Coupons: Offer limited-time discounts, coupon codes, or special bundle deals to entice buyers.
- Free Shipping Promotions: Attract budget-conscious buyers by offering free shipping on specific items or purchases above a certain amount.
- Clearance Sales: Get rid of slow-moving inventory with strategic clearance sales at discounted prices.
- Bundle Offers: Group complementary products at a discounted price to encourage higher order values.
- Contests and Giveaways: Generate excitement and engagement by hosting contests or giveaways related to your products.

Conclusion

From Garage Sale Guru to Global Gemstone Giant: The Inspiring Story of Sarah Jones and "Sparkling Gems"

The Spark Ignites: Sarah Jones, a stay-at-home mom with a passion for gemstones, started "Sparkling Gems" as a humble hobby, selling unique pieces at local garage sales. Recognizing the potential of online marketplaces, she ventured onto eBay, initially listing a handful of items with captivating photos and detailed descriptions.

Lesson #1: Passion ignites opportunity. Pursue what you love, and the drive to succeed will follow.

From Local to Global: Sarah's meticulous attention to detail, her commitment to sourcing ethically mined stones, and her genuine customer service resonated with buyers worldwide. Soon, "Sparkling Gems" expanded beyond garage sales, garnering a loyal following on eBay and building a global customer base.

Lesson #2: Authenticity and quality resonate. Invest in ethically sourced products and exceptional customer service to build trust and loyalty.

Embracing Challenges: As her business flourished, Sarah faced challenges. Managing inventory growth, keeping up with international shipping regulations, and navigating online competition demanded constant learning and adaptation.

Lesson #3: Challenges are inevitable, but growth lies in embracing them. Embrace lifelong learning and adapt your strategies to stay ahead of the curve.

Building an Empire: Today, "Sparkling Gems" is a thriving online empire, employing a team and fulfilling orders worldwide. Sarah actively participates in industry events, mentors aspiring sellers, and advocates for ethical sourcing practices.

Lesson #4: Success breeds responsibility. Give back to the community, share your knowledge, and contribute to a better future for your industry.

The Glimmering Takeaway: Sarah's journey is a testament to the power of passion, dedication, and continuous learning. By focusing on quality, ethical practices, and exceptional customer service, she transformed a garage sale hobby into a globally recognized business. Remember, the road to success isn't always smooth, but with the right mindset and unwavering passion, you too can turn your spark into a shining success story on eBay.

I hope this story inspires you on your own eBay journey!

Made in the USA
Columbia, SC
11 June 2024

36963160R00065